SILENT TEARS

By

TOM GILLESPIE

ISBN: 9798781330720

Printed in the United States of America

Published by Book Marketeers.com

"O father, Lord of Heaven and earth, Thank you for hiding the truth from those who think themselves so wise and for revealing it to little children."

Matthew 11:25

TABLE OF CONTENTS

JANUARY 1947 – MARCH 1947

The air outside was a bone chilling cold. January was a harsh month. The skies were clear, a horse and wagon were making their way up the street. A mother was dressing one of three boys for Sunday School. She slid over his clothes, a blue jumpsuit, which completely enclosed his small body. Her son had just turned five on the 18th and as a result, a happy birthday song would be sung for him in church.

Nashville was just beginning to recover from a recession following World War II. Many goods were still transferred by horse and wagon. In this part of Nashville, the poor whites earned a meager living. Very few cars ware available to this class of people, and buses were the backbone of transportation. As the three boys waved goodbye to their mother, they left with the local neighbors' girls. One girl just fifteen, the younger one twelve. They walked for a half mile to the small block church. On the inside, classrooms were divided by wooden shutters; wooden row seats lined the room, not covered by felt as the other churches. A small church, but newly built.

Tommy punched Judy in the ribs and asked, "When are they going to sing Happy Birthday to me?"

Judy was a slim built girl, her long blond hair swirled as she turned toward Tommy. "Honey," she said in a whisper," I forgot to tell the Preacher." I'll buy you a present tomorrow and sing to you myself."

After church was over, Tommy didn't notice his brothers, Gerald, one and a half years older, and Donald, one year younger, were running ahead of group. He was stunned, his big moment shattered by not hearing his song.

They crossed Humphries Street to a small row house of three rooms. Each room was heated by coal burning fire places. A big potbellied stove sat in the center of the middle room. As Tommy entered, he glanced up at his mother.

"They forgot to sing happy birthday to me!" Tommy was shedding tears. His mother hugged him gently and lifted him gently upon the small wooden table to undress him. As she unzipped the jumpsuit Tommy felt a distraction from the corner of the room. He glanced around, past the three straight back chairs, and sitting in the only real piece of furniture, a reclining chair, was a small thin man. He had receding gray hair and wore wire rimmed glasses. On his small frame was a heavy brown overcoat that hung to the floor.

"Brother Christian, this is my middle son, Tommy. It seems he's a little disappointed. I believe they didn't sing Happy Birthday to him in Church, today."

"Well Tommy, we'll never forget," he replied in a strong baritone voice, Tommy was stunned by his deep voice, and it came from such a little man.

The moment was broken when Gerald and Donald were changed and ready to play outside. All three boys scampered out of the house, down the wooden side porch and into the yard.

SILENT TEARS

Brother Christian remained in the house a few minutes more saying his good-byes to Mrs. Gillespie. As he passed Tommy to get into his car, both eyed the other, Tommy not knowing the meaning of his words, "We'll never forget"

As the days passed the daily chores of living continued. A horse drawn ice wagon churned its way up the street stopping at the houses with their ice signs out. The iceman chopped at a large block until a smaller piece separated, and with huge claws, would latch onto the smaller block and place them into the houses. Most homes still had iceboxes. Besides an icebox, the Gillespie's also had a wood burning cook stove. The children took bathes in a twenty-gallon wash tub. At night, a small white room pot was used to keep from making a trip to the little house out back.

The children's father had fought in the war. He returned at times in a uniform. Their memories of him faded as their mother showered great love on them.

Sundays came and went and, on each Sunday, came new adventures, and every once in a while, a friend, who was sporting a 1938 Chevy. Trips on Sunday were increasing and in particular trips outside of Nashville.

On one of the Sunday trips, the car driven by Bob White (a local bar owner) entered through two square brick post having a sign which read "Tennessee Baptist Orphanage Home". Of course, the children could not read or care where they were going. This was only one of few pleasures they had.

Upon entering through the posts, big red brick buildings abounded. A small paved road wound its way through several of the buildings, which were three stories high. Each building was situated on about a two-acre lot.

Piano music was coming from one. "One of these days you boys will be playing that music," the mother said. Her remarks were hardly noticed as all three small heads were pressed against the car windows, trying to grasp in their tiny minds a place so huge and looming.

Over the next five years they would learn slowly and painfully every building here. Ignorant of this fact, they enjoyed this rare Sunday outing.

MARCH 1947 – JUNE 1947

"Kids, let's go for a ride." The words of a mother in love with each echoed. The kids scampered into Bob White's '38 Chevy and again were ready for new adventures. The afternoon chill hung in the still air and not a cloud was in the sky. After a few hours of driving around the kids found themselves once more driving through the big posts where the large buildings abounded. As they rounded a curve the car went into a circular driveway with hedges on both sides and stopped at the front door. What a place to play hide-and-seek.

"Mother, hold my hand," said Tommy as they walked from the car and into the large building.

She led her son into a large corridor in the middle of the building, then into a room directly to the right 3rd to 1st person. I'll never forget big picture of men wearing bright red coats, riding fast and furious on horses as they were brandishing swords and going into battle, I twisted my head around from my chair to study this strange picture. I was to later see and marvel over this picture many times.

Mother was talking to a woman dressed in white. I'd paid little attention to them. Someone further down the corridor had opened a door, revealing sounds of kids playing, laughing and just making all kinds of noise. Each of us were itching to go join the party.

SILENT TEARS

After a period of time mother embraced each of us and said she'd be back later. "This is going to be your babysitter; I want all of you boys to behave yourselves."

Mother had often left us with babysitters, and though this was rather a large and unusual house, we didn't really mind. We were anxious to explore the other room.

As mother left the woman in white took us straight to the large room and we couldn't believe our eyes. There were more toys here than we had ever seen before. We indulged immediately and for hours we were in another world. Darkness fell and the babysitter fed us until we could eat no more. Then we were served orange jello, and we forced ourselves to eat a few bites more. After supper we were given baths and with other children at this enormous house, we were put to bed. There were three to four beds in each room. All of them had stiff white sheets and everything was sparkling clean.

As we later found out this big house was the hospital and our "babysitter" was a registered nurse. She and her aids were well trained in thoughtfulness for the occupants. This was a very up to date hospital, with clean well-lit hallways and lots of windows. Everything except the playroom stayed immaculate, even the yard.

I snuggled into bed, as tired as I could ever remember being. We had played with few interruptions, and made lots of new friends. Gerald and I had un decided, while we were undressing, that we would tell Mother how much we liked this babysitter so she would let us stay again sometime.

The next morning Mother had not come to get us yet, but we weren't too worried. We ate, and then played some more. Occasionally one of the members of the staff would come in and give a kid a physical examination, which they made into a game.

The nurse and the rest of the girls that completed their staff were masters of manipulation. They were all very loving because they knew what would happen later; they knew what this institution was. In fact, the girls who helped the staff were members, as we now were, of this home.

Several days passed with the only change being the menu. We still weren't worried about Mother picking us up, she had always picked us up before. We didn't cry and we didn't complain much, but Gerald and I decided that if Mother would bring us back to this big house again, we would ask her to come get us sooner next time.

In later years I understood the indoctrination period. First, children were brought to the hospital for a physical examination and while they played, a mental observation was made. In three to five days, they were assigned to a building, according to sex and age.

On about the fifth day, Donald and I were moved to the "baby building". This building was occupied by children through the age of about seven, depending on when their birthdays fell. This was the only building in which girls and boys resided together casually. The bathrooms weren't even segregated. It was also the only building that housed its own cafeteria and a special playroom, but here the matron, Mrs. Bartwell, wasn't loving and caring. She and her helpers, the older girls, were regimented in affection, and none of them had patience with screaming kids. They were just nice not exceptionally nice, as long as everyone behaved and they didn't have to attend to us very often.

At first Donald and I didn't miss Gerald at all. Events were too confusing and everything was moving too fast. I was trying to understand why Mother had forgotten to come after me. Late one afternoon, as I was swinging, I spied the hospital. This, I reasoned, must be it! Mother hadn't gotten us yet because the babysitter had moved us to this other building. I jumped from the swing, trying to keep the hospital in sight, and started in a dead run straight for that building. The distance from the hospital to the baby building was greater than I thought, but I ran every step of the way that day, my little legs carrying me as fast as they could. I bolted in and down the hall, straight for the playroom, a secured area. Someone caught me from behind and asked me a few questions then allowed me to play in the room and sleep over night in the hospital. The next morning, without explanation, I was once again moved to the baby building.

It happened quite often during the next two weeks, but I was always returned to the baby building. The last time I was making a hospital run, instead of the adults stopping me, I was stopped by kids my own age. They held me down and explained, or tried to explain the best they could, what had happened. I was shattered but I tried to settle down to their way of life. During the hospital runs I remembered little of the other events or activities. Now I became accustomed to a serviceable routine.

March or April Through July 47

Baby Building

In the bay building there were many rooms. In one long room were piles and piles of long john underwear. The matron, who was mother, headmaster, teacher, and disciplinarian stopped me in front of a pile and began holding up different sizes to my body until she saw a match. With four pairs of long johns four or five shirts and overalls I was sent to the shoe room. An ankle high pair of shoes and some socks completed my wardrobe. Everyone looked the same here. Our haircuts were as identical as were our clothes… all were obviously practical, disgustingly identical.

It was sill winter in Nashville, so our days were spent confined to the playroom. When the noisy games and screams and laughter became unbearable all of us were lined up and made to sit in the room along the wall for hours without a sound. This happened quite often during the winter months. But with spring coming we were able to play outside most days and this greatly relieved the matron and her helpers but especially the children. One Sunday Donald and I were playing outside and one of the girls told us to go inside to the living room. We had never even been allowed in that room before so we were quite confused at being asked to go there. We walked slowly trying to remember everything we'd done and if we could possibly be in trouble for something. As we entered the room all our worst fears were relieved.

"Mother Mother" we cried. "Are we going home now?"

There was no time to answer as hugging and kissing engulfed the first half hour.

"Look what I have brought for ya'll!" Mother opened a bag filled with toys and candy. We grabbed them and dug around in them squealing with laughter, since candy had not been in our diet.

"Mama, we only see Gerald when he walks to supper at the big building."

"Sometimes we can talk to him when we're playing. Are you going to get him too?"

Questions galore.

Mama, we're ready to go home now. Mama why did you leave us for so long?

Mother stood transfixed, still as a statue. After what seemed an eternity, she turned back to us.

"I must go now, but I'll be back and I'll see you all together next time. I'll sure miss my boys. I've already seen Gerald today and I must go."

We began crying and pleading.

Mama Mama Mama don't leave us here again. Take us with you. Mama please don't leave us. Don't leave.

SILENT TEARS

Mother stood on the porch gazing into our eyes. She stroked my cheek and finally said she would come back sooner next time. We cried for another hour at least.

After that time, we always got together as a family, and soon Mother tried to explain to us about the money problem and why she couldn't afford to keep us at home with her. Instead of all of us living in poverty she had chosen to have it this way.

Her sisters had offered to separate us and raise us in their homes, but Mother had not been able to bear to lose her children this way. The only other practical alternative was the orphanage. She had to secure her family from hunger and thirst.

Toward the first summer a new survival trend started. I later found out it had been going on for years. If one kid knew another had done something that an older kid would whip him for, he would hold it against him in order to get favors.

We were small time blackmailers. When the victim's mother would come to see him and give him candy or toys, they would say, "give it to me or I will tell on you." This would go on for days, weeks or months. In order to break the hold, the victim had to watch for hours, hoping and waiting. When finally, the holder did something he could get into trouble for the hold was broken. On couldn't tell so that the other wouldn't.

In the upstairs portion of the baby building there were sleeping dorms. There were large rooms with sometimes twenty beds to a room. At night the hall lights were left on and a radio was tuned to WSM's Grand Old Opry. In our group was a very popular girl named Unise Dean Duke. It's now hard to believe, but at the tender age of seven this girl had learned about the birds and bees, and had set out on a mission to teach all the boys about them too. Her reputation got around and at night boys from other floors would be lined up to meet Unise Dean under a bed by the door.

Her idea of a screw was to let a BOY LAY ON HER AND TOUCH HER FOR SEVERAL MINUTES. Of course, no one really learned at this age why or how to really operate, but knew where each part was to go, thanks to Unise Dean. Unise Dean wasn't too smart at homework and such, but she had more toys and got more candy than any other kid in the building.

One Sunday, before the mother of one particular boy left, she went to the restroom and Unise Dean had her boy under the bed next to the living room… poor Unise Dean.

THE BASEMENT

A source of control over the kids at night was to march the ones making noise to the basement. Fear was used as a tool of obedience. All kids were told a witch was in the basement. One of the matrons' helpers opened the basement door at the top of a stairwell and another pushed all the kids in. The light inside was controlled outside the door. Instantly in went out. Like an animal on the run, a wild fear swept the kids. Other girls were at the bottom of the steps, moaning and reaching her hand up through the steps. The yells of terror could be heard throughout the other floors. Not a single kid left the stairwell without wetting our messing in their clothes. They would tremble for the rest of the night, afraid of sleep.

AUGUST 1948 END OF SUMMER

PLAYING

We were playing on the merry go round in front of the baby building when two boys about my age were walking along the long sidewalk in front of the main cafeteria toward the little boys building. One of the hospital girls was with them... Here were two new kids and I thought I knew how they felt.

"What's ya'lls names?" I yelled out to them.

Don and Wayne Hawkins were the answer. At first, I noticed a slight difference in their attitude. A more open and not afraid look. Almost a happy one. This puzzled me and I walked around thinking how strange they were.

About this time Bobby Brewer walked up asking me if I wanted to see something new.

"Sure " I said. "Show me."

As I stood in anticipation, hoping to learn more of his famous but not too well working tricks. He took a piece of string and told me to wrap it around my finger. I did this without questioning. "Okay, now pull it tight and watch your finger turn purple."

I did and it did, boy how it worked! I had a purple fingertip. "How did you learn that?" I questioned.

Bobby pointed to the older boys in the field, holding down a calf." They were doing it to that baby bull."

"How come they want to turn that bull purple?"

"I don't know. They said the purple would fall off."

I released the string; I knew I didn't want to live without a finger.

1948 Probably around August

School starts

Summer was coming to a close and I was looking forward to going to school. A child that becomes an orphan finds few pleasures in growing up. School was a pleasant change in life.

The school was run by matrons, some had teaching degrees or some sort of formal education Kindergarten, first, and second grades were more or less an extension of playing. We drew pictures, heard stories, and learned a little about acceptable classroom behavior.

The teachers were entirely new to us, and it gave us a feeling of elation to know that five days of the week we would go to see these new friends of ours. Most children started some kind of mother and child relationship with one or more of the women. The teachers who were new really had their work cut out for them. After Mrs. Bartwell and the helpers at the baby building any sort of kindness was responded to with a kind of glee most of them could never understand. A loving smile or a soft touch and any child there would gladly be a slave for the rest of the year.

In kindergarten I was up with the sun. After breakfast, I threw on coat of my friends and ran to the building that served as church and school.

After school if the weather permitted, we played outside. On occasion we could smell salted ham cooking, a smell that would associate itself with the orphanage for the remainder of my lifetime.

Going to school had provided a real escape into another world with the expansion of the mind instilled with fairy tales, nights were easier with far away dreams into a world where no hurt or pain could be felt

That winter snow was at least a foot deep and it seemed forever to melt as spring came with fresh scents of flowers. and a cool breeze to cross your face.

I knew soon I would be transferred to the little boys building and could be with Gerald. Rumors were circulating as to who would go in the summer. This excitement was more than enough to hold me through nights screams of terror from the basement and running to sit around the playroom wall.

School came to a close and I was now six years old.

Summer was a time to bring biscuits and peanut butter cookies outside after lunch and sit under a tree as you munched while watching the tractors plowing the fields.

About May/June

1949

AUGUST 1949

One summer morning, I awoke thinking at once that today was the day to move to the little boys building. Gerald would know that I would be coming and it was great knowing that I would now spend some time with my older brother. Five of us were making the move: Bobby Brewer, Gary Richardson, George Howard, Billy Tilsdale, and myself. Donald, of course, wouldn't make this move for at least another year. All of these boys had experienced the pains such as of severe unhappiness while at the baby building. Bobby Brewer like myself was looking forward to seeing an older brother in the little boys building. We knew when we entered this building that it was much larger than the baby building.

There were two regular stories, and then an attic with at least eight beds. A full basement with two large long tables mounted into a cement floor. Also in the basement were a row of benches around the wall... The regular stories had three sleeping rooms. The west room had three beds, the middle room had three beds and the east room at least ten beds. On the second floor the matron had her quarters.

We were led up the stairs to Mrs. Barton's room. When we entered, she appeared the grandmother type. At first, we were given instructions as to what and what not to do, where and where not to go but We hardly paid attention. We wanted to play and, explore our new "yard"' luckily Mrs. Barton had a few other things on her mind and she dismissed us for a while, to go outside to the large back yard. At least two acres, all the running space a child needed. Since, we were new, the kids all gathered around us telling us who had built the greatest sled and how fast it could go. Sleds for the summer. Small sled-looking stands with runners smoothed down by pulling them over the grass. A few kids were showing them of demonstration how they worked. All at once all five of us were hanging on for dear life going down the hill behind the older boys. As the sled I was on whipped by a boy, a piece of wood from the runner sticking out like a knife went through his leg. He fell to the ground. in pain, writhing in apparent agony. Everyone gathered around not quite knowing how to help, and the Mrs. Barton came out. I was standing farther away and watched her, rather than help the boy up, she twisted his ear and slapped him in the face and yelled "how could you let this happen!" She whipped him repeatedly as he hobbled to the hospital

During the thirty or so minutes of Mrs. Bartons absence the older kids went on a rampage: yelling, running through the cornfield, and down into the basement knocking out windows with broom handles. To me it was quite an air of excitement. I didn't know what to do but yell with everyone, Gerald put his hand over my mouth to quiet me as he tried to explain the anger in the group. It's a new life and would be hard to accept If I didn't keep my mouth shut or if I told on the other boys I would probably get beat up.

His words only stayed with me as long as it took him to say them but we sat down in the yard and watched what seemed to smoothed be a great show unknown to me. Gerald was protecting me by letting the other matrons coming to stop the racket know we weren't doing anything. As the matrons and older boys from the big boys building started rounding up this mob, I noticed Richard

Brewer had Bobby sitting down next to him. In fact, quite a few boys were sitting down just watching. Most of the noise makers were the older boys of this building. Night came late and we were assigned rooms and beds. I was in the same room as Gerald in fact the influx of new residents was such that I was to sleep with Gerald. I jumped straight into bed and noticed Gerald was folding and straightening his clothes. Where he picked this up, I never learned.

Before we could get to sleep the whippings started. Everyone involved was lined up. Each kid was marched to a chair and made to bend over. The leather strap Mrs. Barton wielded sounded like a whip cracking. She gave them all twenty licks each. Most of them could hardly walk. Some of them danced around and some fell to the ground after their whipping. I laid there frozen as the whippings were taking place in the middle of our room. Any other matron was on hand in case a kid wanted to rebel. By this time, all their energy had been used up during the raid on the building. If a kid was sitting crying out loud after the lights went out, Mrs. Barton would give them a few extra licks to silence them.

At last, the building was quiet and I could see the WSM radio tower out my window, the raid light flashing on and off. I was tired and scared.

The next few weeks were a learning process. We found out who in the building could whip everybody else then on down the line for about fifteen boys. The lower twenty had to fight among themselves for position in rank. Being still new in the little boys building everybody left us five new kids alone until we were in the rank and file some kids showed us their secrets in hope of winning new friends. One of the secrets was the cornfield which was loaded with hiding place. The Olman farm "next to the orphanage" was the home of a wealthy construction company owner. It contained some of the best Tennessee walking horses in the country. A large garden for stealing raw vegetables on an excursion trip was another of many recuts of exploration, was new and exciting. Still the first night of tension was rooted in my mind. I received no whippings for a long time.

SUMMER & SCHOOL - 1949

During the summer at the little boys building there was always something going on. One day in the cornfield Gerald asked me if I wanted some parched corn.

"What is it?" I asked.

With that he built a small fire and found a tin can. He then broke off an ear of corn and put the kernels into the can. The corn did not pop but burnt almost to a pop. We ate our fill and what a rare treat it was. In the middle of the cornfield, we felt hidden from the world, but when you see smoke, a fire is not far behind. To our dismay, Mrs. Barton was observing from the second-floor window. She could see no kids in the field but she could see smoke from several fires. She did what seemed to be her favorite hobby in the summertime. She rang a small bell and began to call the roll.

All the kids ran from different parts of the yard to the little boys building under the last windows. As we left the field Gerald showed me how to find a tree in line with her field of view and walk toward the tree until in the yard. As we gathered under the window my heart was pounding. What excitement not to be caught. As we looked around, I noticed about three boys missing from our group. Boys I thought are they going to get it! As Mrs. Barton read the roll about ten boys down, the name of Bill Smotherman came up. I knew he was missing but as she read his name, I heard a "here" come from the far side of the crowd; as I looked up in amazement and shock,

Gerald yanked my arm, indicating for me to look back and not to move. In fact, I was surprised that everybody answered. I could have sworn about three boys were missing. I was right. Three boys answered twice. The system was becoming clearer to me.

As we walked back to the yard, Bill Smotherman came from the cornfield not knowing that roll had been called. Mrs. Barton was still at her perch. "Bill Smotherman, come here."

As he walked toward the building, every time he passed a tree, kids were handing him paper and rags. Then they did, he would stuff his pockets with them or the seat of his pants. This would soften the blows of her belts. The whisperings for being in the cornfield were not as bad as others. But Bill wanted all the odds in his favor. Boy to hear him yell, you would think it was his first. What an actor! Later Bill had to come outside and stand on the sidewall holding one foot up. As he faced the yard, he made faces and we knew who got who.

As summer passed, we prepared for school. Every kid had a benefactor or church whose donations were to keep them clothed as long as they were in the orphanage.

The orphanage was run by the Southern Baptist Church. We received the church's teachings day and night. We went to prayer meetings on Wednesday night, Sunday school, church and training union on Sunday, and every day during school, a small church service, before classes.

The Baptists really made us believe God was one of them. They tried to pull the fear of God in us, not knowing Mrs. Barton as well as we did. The fear of her was more than that of the devil.

SILENT TEARS

September 1949 1st Grade

School was exciting as the new term began and we could again mix and walk to the girls. I even had my eye on a certain Joan Davis. My first heart throb.

That summer all the boys had girlfriends. As far as puppy love went at that age to stare a cross to their yard and to get one to stare back was the thing. I had my eyes on Mary Joan Worthy, but Ralph McCarty, who become a friend, told me she had hair in her legs. She was dark complected and the hairs showed up more than the other girls. I quickly dropped the idea of her, but twenty years later when I was able to meet her in a Nashville, I discovered that sometimes hairy legged girls grew up and became beautiful women who learned how to shave their legs, Mary Joan Worthy had the legs. Mary Joan also had everything else. I revealed that story to her and we both laughed at the years so long passed.

RALPH TRIES – FALL OR WINTER 1949 OR 1950

One rainy night while we were confined to the basement playroom, I noticed ten small boys next to the east wall with three larger boys standing guard, and not letting them leave. A few other boys were going through the group of small boys left picking a few more. They did not pick me or Gerald. As one of them passed us he said to another larger boy, "the Gillespies had done nothing to hunt them." After about fifteen smaller boys had been chosen, they were led (one by one) to the larger boy that had been offended by some small erk the little boy had done. The larger boy then beat the younger boy about the face as hard as he could swing. After about five or six kids were beaten up in this manner the larger boy plowed into those left, hurrying punches and blasts to the smaller boys, before Mrs. Barton came down the find out what was happening. A lookout boy ran into the basement and yelled a warning. Everything broke up as if nothing had happened. The smaller boys sniffled or moaned a little but did not cry openly. Mrs. Barton asked what all the screaming was about, but no one dared tell for fear of a new beating.

That night I asked Gerald why the smaller boys had been beaten up. I was afraid I would be beaten because in the baby building, we all told off but nothing like this ever took place. That night I slept close to my brother, not knowing who to fear most, Mrs. Barton or the older boys. The next morning one of the smaller boys beaten up was missing. Ralph McCarty was a tough kid; he took the beating but didn't cry of scream. I noticed his eye swelling as we had gotten into bed the night before.

"McCarty has run away!" Someone yelled and the news spread to Mrs. Barton. A new wave of excitement came over the whole building. Ralph had defied the system and left on his own... Wet footprints pointed toward the railroad tracks where trains had to slow down going up a grade. McCarty had jumped a train to Nashville. Ralph was found two days later in Nashville begging for food and returned to the orphanage. He was treated like a hero by all the boys; big and little. The older boys found a new respect for him because he had accomplished something they never had. Defied Authority. Mrs. Barton kept Ralph confined that day to the building. That night as we washed up for supper, a chair was place in the middle of the basement. We were marched into the basement and told to line up on the benches according to height. As we sat there Mrs. Barton brought Ralph McCarty in without a shirt on. She had a razor strap. We felt what was coming. "You kids" she said, "remember what you see here as I'm sure Ralph will." She laid him over the chair and whipped his back and butt until whelps burst through the skin and bled. He finally cracked and began screaming to the top of his lungs until he fainted. I hadn't noticed but my hand was squeezing the hand of the kid next to me. His fingers were turning blue. He yelled from my squeezes.

"Douglas what is wrong with you!" she yelled.

"Tommy was hurting my hand."

SILENT TEARS

Mrs. Barton walked toward me and seemed to be the largest thing on earth as she neared me. Her eyes were as if a devil lived in her.

She drew back the razor strap and swung it across my legs deadening them for a few seconds. I screamed out but no sound came out until I was patted on the back by Douglas. How I yelled then. "Shut up or I'll whip you again." I didn't know what shut my mouth but it closed and not another sound did it make.

"All right now remember what you saw tonight and remember what you say. Now go to supper."

I could barely walk. Gerald helped me in the long march to the cafeteria about a block away. Ralph McCarty did not go for supper that night. He was only seven years old.

REVENGE

Bobby Moon could whip every kid in our building. Bobby was a quiet boy, and kept to himself. He was raised from five years old at the orphanage and was an insider. After World War II many older kids from the streets of Nashville's slums were left at the orphanage while their parents got a new start. These kids stayed for two to three years then went to a new home. These type kids brought "the system" to the building. They knew street talk and knew how to fight. Jessie Stewart was an outsider. Jessie was second up the ladder and around him was a small clan of hanger-ons. A small time hood. These were the bearers of smaller kids. I never saw Bobby Moon beat anyone but I have seen him fight. Moon played a harmonica and Gerald was a friend of his. Gerald could not always protect me from the older kids.

Once I had talked to Jessie's girlfriend and did what little boys did, pull her hair and chunk some rocks at her, and in general just irritated the hell out of her. All this in route to the school. At school work got to Jessie and that night after supper I noticed a guard being placed at the door again and felt the uneasiness in the air.

Stewart and his hoods started picking out kids to feel their wrath. To my amazement I was picked and was told I should not have talked to his girlfriend. Gerald started acting frantic. He could not protect me or he would also feel the blows.

While we, the chosen ones, were huddled in a group waiting the start, Gerald pleaded with Stewart not to hurt me. Stewart's ego had been bruised. He could not break down unless the others would think less of him as a leader. Ralph McCarty was also in my group. He was unafraid, or seemed to be. He grabbed my arm and told me to put my hands over my face, fall on the first blow and double up into a knot. This would keep the punishment to a minimum. As the other kids watched I received the first hit. It was unexpected as the older kids kept us off guard saying they would hit us with belts on the butts and only two licks. I got an instant headache; tears began to flow freely from my eyes and I staggered around like a punching bag swaying but not allowed to all to the floor. I could see through this punishment and remember tears in Gerald's eyes more than my beating. He felt the pain and Moon could see this also. After a few more hits to my midsection Moon stepped in and told them to let me 80. I felt lucky, the other kids were still feeling the blows for a few more minutes. That night in bed Gerald tried to comfort me and tried to assure me that he would try to keep this from happening again. Ralph McCarty came to my bed beside me and smiling, told me he wasn't hurt.

"Hey Tommy, " he whispered, "you want to help me get these guys back for that?"

"Well sure, I want to get them back, just like everyone else but no one can beat them up," I whispered back.

"I can, and if you will help, we'll do it tonight, after everyone has gone to sleep."

I thought about this for a minute. I thought about Ralph being the only kid I knew who had run clean away from the orphanage and made it all the way to Nashville, on a train.

SILENT TEARS

"O.K., Ralph, what do you want me to do?"

"You just wait till I come back tonight and wake you up, then you follow me, and I'll tell you what to do then." Ralph got back on the floor and snuck back to his bed.

I rolled onto my back and just thought awhile about how tough this kid was, and felt all the confidence I needed growing and building inside me. I drifted to sleep thinking about how two little guys like us were going to get back at those big guys, probably snoring in my sleep.

"Wake up Tommy " Ralph was at my side again shaking me to consciousness." Follow me."

In a bound I was out of bed following him downstairs to the first-floor dormitory. In the first beds were two of the beaters. Jessie Stewart was in another room so we decided not to take a chance on his revenge.

"What can we do to them, Ralph?" I asked. They'll know who we are when they wake up."

Don't worry, they won't see us, and they won't get us back this time," Ralph assured me. I could hear the anger in his voice as we neared out zero point. Bobby Moon was in this room and we could not wake him up. "Don't worry, " Ralph sand I have a good plan." He was creeping without a sound, and I began to fear for my incompetence. "We're going to get them so bad; they'll never think of beating us again."

Ralph went to the linen closet and pulled out two sheets. He was explaining my part of the plan to me. "Unfold the sheet over their heads."

I thought this would really scare them good. They'd wake up and it would be so dark they'd think they were dead, or smothering to death. "After that, you just run out of the room and wait for me."

Why wait? I wondered. It was a real puzzlement to me. We crawled into the room on our stomachs and the floor creaked as if the building was settling. All the kids were in a deep sleep and I wished I was too. As we crawled past Bobby Moon's bed, I was behind Ralph, and when I turned to look toward Moon my heart sank. He was awake! I couldn't move. Here I was on the floor about one o'clock in the morning with a sheet and the toughest kid in the building staring me in the eye.] finally moved forward and Moon rose a little to see what was going on. Ralph was totally unaware we were being watched. When we approached beds, I had wet my pants from fear that the Moon look had put in me. Moon was laying down and I could see his face was looking toward us. It was too late now I couldn't tell Ralph and I couldn't back out. We unfolded the sheets and pulled them up over the head boards. We both stood up and there was hardly room for one person between the beds. Ralph placed me in front of him toward the entrance. He raised his hands and gave both sheets to me to pull.

All I had to do was pull the sheets and run. I thought he was going to scare them. He gave the signal and I pulled with all my might. The sheet fell over the punks' heads but did not awake them. I was on a dead run and Ralph stood there looking down. As I got to the door Ralph drew back his fist and hit both boys (who were still in bed) between the legs. Their screams could be heard throughout the buildings and as everybody awoke, I was in bed looking up with the rest of the kids. Mrs. Barton sprang from her room.

"What are you kids doing?"

SILENT TEARS

"Playing with the sheets." how,

She was furious! Both of those kids got an additional beating. It was daybreak before my heart stopped beating so fast. As we washed up the next morning, I was again looking Bobby Moon in the eyes. Fear again swept over me for I knew at any moment I would be getting a beating. After what seemed an eternity to me, Moon smiled and walked out. That breakfast was extra good, as was my mood!

Should be September + October 1949

Trick or Treat

"Tommy I'm going to run away again! I know how to do it now, I have a plan, and I've got a map of Tennessee!"

"Ralph, she'll beat you again if you get caught."

"I ain't gonna get caught again."

This conversation went on during playtime at school. The schoolhouse also doubled as a church. It had classrooms, a large auditorium, a band room downstairs. The schoolhouse was three stories high and resembled all the other buildings, but also all brick schools of those days. We were in another world at school and enjoyed going. Here we could talk and didn't have to look over our shoulders.

"Oh, look at those flowers!"

"What kind are they?"

"Snap-dragons," Ralph replied. "Look Tommy!" As Ralph pulled one, he held it in his hands and with his thumb and forefinger pressed the bud and it looked like a puppet as it opened its mouth.

Our teacher noticed our interest and didn't scold us for picking the flower, but explained how it was planted and the care needed for it. Miss Riley became the closest thing to an angel we knew. Newer was she harsh or loud. As we went back into the classroom Ralph said, "I planned this one and nothing will go wrong," want to go with me?"

"I don't know, Gerald and Donald are still here and mother comes to see us. If we got lost, I'd never see her again."

"Yeah, I guess you're right, I don't have a Mother or Daddy though."

Halloween was coming on and the kids tied cord between the large columns over the benches and hung cut-outs of owls, witches, ghosts, and so on. It looked pretty good and created a different atmosphere.

It seemed like Halloween was a favorite time of the older kids in our buildings and the thing was to play a trick on Mrs. Barton and not feel her revenge. A window breaking out as she laid in bed, her bed falling down, a slip on an over waxed floor. The fire alarm going off without anyone in the hallway, we thought, would be the best plan. We had to figure out how to do it. Every Thursday night at 7:30 Mrs. Barton's treat to us was to let us listen to the Gene Autry Radio Show. We sat in the hallway around her room and Mrs. Barton put her radio into the hall. She left her door open and we all listened to "Back in the Saddle Again". For thirty minutes we were all back out West.

But as each Thursday got closer to Halloween, I noticed more conversation being paid to the fire bell next to her room. A large black clang type bell, with a wire pull string hanging down to about two feet from the floor. We had a few drills and the bell could rock the building. Bobby Moon and Jessie Stewart teamed up for this try and everyone was giving ideas as to how it could be done. No one yet could find a way without getting someone caught. One day Bird nest Hawkins came up with the answer. "Why don't someone just sleepwalk??" He asked. "I do it all the time. Mrs. Barton had even caught me a couple of times, and just slaps me awake."

Moon perked up. "You know Bird nest, it might work. And since Mrs. Barton knows you sleepwalk, You're it."

Now Hawkins knew he should have kept his mouth shut. He could not back out, Jessie Stewart promised him a beating if he did. Bill Hawkins was his real name and when he came to the little boys building, he had short bushy hair in a neat ball piled on top of his head. His first night at the building and kids made fun of his looks that might about how he had a bird nest on top. Of course, he cried to Mrs. Barton. She in turn whipped him to make him shut up and he got his nickname, Bird nest.

Bird nest's room was in the attic above the floor with the alarm and during the day when Mrs. Barton went to see a matron in the other building Bird nest practiced his sleepwalk and pulled the bell without ringing it. Of course, he became an instant hero and with the encouragement of the older boys Bird nest could have walked through fire and believed he wouldn't be hurt. He even made two or three dry runs down the hall so Mrs. Barton would wake him up believing he was sleepwalking. This was to reinforce his routine for Halloween night. Ralph, Gerald and I all talked about running away, where to go, and how to do it, but we also were building up our hopes of Mrs. Bartons fright of the fire alarm going off while in a dead sleep.

SILENT TEARS

Halloween came and that night in the main cafeteria, a few larger boys wore masks, we had Halloween candy and heard a few ghost stories, including the story of the Bell Witch of Tennessee (which drew some chuckles from the group from the Little Boys Building.). As we walked back to our building during the dark of night, we could all feel the goblins. Everyone knew the hour of twelve was the time. No one slept and in every room a watch or clock was being monitored. At midnight we could hear the creaking of the steps giving under the weight of Bird nest. My muscles were drawing tight and I became stiff as a board awaiting the alarm to go off. I grabbed my mattress and squeezed it until my hand turned blue just knowing what was going to happen. The footsteps grew louder and how Mrs. Barton slept I don't know. I believe a fly could have walked on the floor and I would have heard it.

Bird nest was coming down the hall now. I looked around, everybody was wide awake, just a few more steps. When is it going to ring? When? Two, three, four, five, six more steps, then CLANG CLANG CLANG CLANG! We all sprang up screaming and yelling. We told him to ring it but this was too much. CLANG CLANG. One ring or two maybe but this was too much. Everybody in the orphanage was going to wake up. CLANG CLANG CLANG CLANG. Finally, he stopped. My ears were ringing. Shouts of older boys from other buildings and matrons rang through out in the night. Brother Christian the superintendent was there. Everyone stared at Hawkins. We were shocked. It was Bird nest's older brother Don, not Bird nest.

He began to yell, "stop the bell, stop the bell, stop the bell!" Brother Christen shook Don gently by the shoulders. Don acted dazed, and Brother Christain embraced him to comfort him, believing the boy was going mad. As we all looked on in disbelief,

Brother Christain led Don out of the building and to the Hospital for some peace and quiet. As quietness settled over the building whispers of what Don had done could be heard until daylight. What a hero he became. Quite smart, and a keeper to himself. A bookworm. But Boy would he get it when he comes back!

Don had put much more thought into this than we had. He would turn thirteen in three days, and he would be transferred to the Big Boys Building. Away from Mrs. Bartons, in fact he didn't even have to come back for a minute. He stayed in the hospital for four days and went straight to the other building from there. He knew what he did and as Mrs. Barton watched him walk by after being released from the hospital, Don yelled, "Hello, Mrs. Barton, CLANG CLANG CLANG." And he ran to the Big Boys Building laughing with the assurance of one who truly has had the last laugh.

AUGUST

"WHEN THE TASSE THE CORN"

Ralph tries too again

Winter came and spring was around the corner. Much of the time was spent studying and sleeping. It became dark around mealtime and free time was hardly a thing to have. As spring approached, we began spring cleaning of the building. I was about seven at the time and a few younger boys under us were now allowed to play while we worked. Gerald and I had to clean the east dormitory where ten beds lined the room. At this time, I had been put in charge of a room as a regular chore. I made all ten beds before going to school. Mrs. Barton checked the room before I could leave the building. All beds were made military style and the sheets and pillows and no wrinkles whatso ever. The floors were dusted every morning. This day, Saturday, was going to be extra hard work. First, we mopped the floors and waited for them to dry. We then put down a paste wax and shined them on hands and knees, with a towel. The whole process took about four hours. Gerald helped me on this Saturday and we talked of far-off places we read about in school. Texas, Arizona, and other places out West. I had written the Austin Chamber of Commerce for a school project and received a picture of a Texas Ranger next to a horse and wearing a cowboy hat. We talked of going over to the big boys building. We knew things were different over there. A man and his wife ran that building and the boys were treated more like men then kids.

, hush and finish this floor," Mrs. Barton was on her
like a well-oiled machine we moved even faster. She
to another room and continued barking orders.

"Gerald," Ralph is going to run away again this summer. He's
got a plan and a map and every day he watches the trains and to find
out what time they are going by."

"Where is he going, to Nashville or to Franklin?"

"I don't know. He's waiting for summer to come so the corn will
be thick and tall."

"I'll tell you, Tommy, he needs to wait until the tassels are on
the corn. Its high then.

We finished the waxing and waited for Mrs. Barton's
inspection.

To our amazement it was clean. "OK, you boys can go now."

That Saturday the noon sun was beaming down warmth and the
slight chill gave us a lazy feeling. We went out into the yard and laid
down, looking at clouds in a blue-sky float by. Jerry and Douglas
Mayers came by and asked was our Mother coming. Sunday. Sure,
Gerald replied, "She comes most Sundays now."

"Our mother will be out too," Jerry said, "she's working now
and maybe soon we'll be leaving."

"For good!" Douglas insisted.

They walked away and Gerald and I looked to the skies again
day dreaming.

"Hi Gerald, hi Tommy, "

SILENT TEARS

"Hey Ralph, lay down," Gerald said. "Tommy told me you're going to run away."

"Yeah, and this time I'll really be gone from here."

" Have you told Don yet?"

"Yeah, he said hold out till I can move over there with him, its better over there he says, but I really don't know if I can wait."

"I can all help the train you," times, replied when Gerald, the Franklin and he began to tell Ralph all the train times, when the Franklin Interurban bus ran and what roads led to where. I just sat there and listened as Gerald poured out the information. My older brother never stopped amazing me with his knowledge. Ralph was even stunned. Gerald read a lot and if we had paid attention, we would have found out he was reading Geography books.

After that day Gerald and Ralph were like two flies on fly paper stuck together. Gerald was furnishing the information and Ralph was furnishing the guts. Word spread like fire throughout the building and helpful hints on how to build fires, where to go in Nashville and how to beg for food came pouring in. It became a united effort. Every boy wished he had the nerve to do it and Ralph became and extension of their hope for a release.

May flew by. Gerald became nine and the com was planted. Summer saw a few more older boys move to the other building and Donald moved to our building. All three together again. I was older myself and had developed a good survival instinct. I didn't receive any more beatings now and the younger boys were learning the new process of not telling on older boys. The older boys now lined middle boys up with each other and had us to fight. At least now we had a chance.

One summer day after lunch Ralph and I were sitting under a tree talking. "The corn is about half grown," I said.

"Yeah, just a few more weeks," replied Ralph.

"Want to walk through the corn field?"

"I don't know, Mrs. Barton might call roll," Ralph answered. "Somebody cover for us?" Someone agreed to, so we went for a look.

At first, we eased into the field and a few paths were already being started for hideouts being staked out. "Let's go to the railroad," yelled Ralph.

"OK lets." We bounded across the field, which seemed to take forever and at the last row lay the tracks. "I hope a train comes by."

"Duck Tommy, Here comes a putt-putt car." We laid down flat as a car with two black men and one white man went by. I became scared, felt like I was in someone else's field.

"Let's go back Ralph."

"Oh, all right," and then, "hey, first let's go by the Oldman's field and get some turnips and tomatoes." Away we went back through the cornfield and down the north tree line. At Oldman's garden we loaded down with cabbage, tomatoes, and turnips. Then we returned to the play yard and divided out the spoils. These were good daytime treats. A few more weeks passed and the tassels were in full bloom. I kept asking Ralph when he was leaving and he just said he was waiting for the right time.

One rainy morning with the air heavy there was a warm mist, one of the little boys came to me and said, "Ralph's gone, and Phil Jenkin is with him."

SILENT TEARS

"Phil Jenkins!" I replied in shock. "I don't believe it." But sure enough, both boys were gone and it didn't take Mrs. Barton long to flash the warning. The air of excitement in the building was at an all-time high. We ate breakfast and was were rushed into the basement and made to sit around the wall and not speak. Of course, we could hardly hold ourselves. Dr. Christain came in and a few matrons came with him. Every boy was questioned. Not one said anything about Ralph. A smaller boy replied he saw Phil get up, dress and walk toward the cafeteria. We knew that if you walked past the cafeteria about a half mile you would come to the Franklin highway and the bus stop. The maintenance man came with Phil about that time and announced his return. Phil's head drooped. Dr. Christain asked him where he was going. "Just home." replied Phil. Phil was a skinny kid with a pair of thick glasses and a high-pitched voice. Standing there he looked like a whipped pup. "Mrs. Barton, please don't whip me!"

" She won't, " said Dr. Christain, "I understand how you feel and I'm sure she does."

Mrs. Barton stood there nodding her head, and inside I'm sure she was steaming waiting her chance. She was boiling like a volcano? After Dr. Christain talked a little bit more to Phil he left with the others to search for Ralph thinking they both took the same route. Actually, Phil had woke up that morning without any knowledge of Ralph's departure. He was homesick and knew the bus went to Nashville. He was eight and had just been in the orphanage for a few months.

"Come here, Phil, " Mrs. Barton said in a low growling voice. As Phil approached her, he thought he would not be punished because of what Dr. Christain had said.

SILENT TEARS

Mrs. Barton laid her hand on his shoulder and grasp his ear with her other hand. "Now tell me where Ralph went."

"I didn't know Ralph was gone."

Mrs. Barton squeezed his ear and began slapping his face.

"WHERE IS HE" she yelled.

"Honest Mrs. Barton, I don't know." Phil was crying out in pain; his face was bright red from the beating. Phil fainted and went to his knees. Mrs. Barton picked him up and slammed him on the bench facing us. We were stunned with horror and she told us not to say a word. When, Phil finally regained his senses Mrs. Barton made him stand on one foot and not move. She made us sit for four hours without going to the bathroom and Phil had to keep his foot up the whole time. At least Mrs. Barton thought he didn't put his foot down. After about half about when she got tired of watching him stand, she left and we stood a guard by the door and told Phil to put his foot down. About every fifteen Minutes she checked to make sure everything was going as it should, and when she looked in Phil had his foot up and we were all sitting silently staring at the walls. When it was absolutely necessary, we urinated into the wash basin so as not to make a noise.

After supper that night we were marched to our bedroom and told not to speak and go straight to bed. It was still daylight and that night our thoughts were with Ralph, who had gotten clean away, and didn't even know the good fortune he had of having a false trail laid out for him.

SILENT TEARS

AUGUST 1949/1950

McCARTY'S ODYSSEY

I worried about Ralph all through the day and night. Where would he sleep? What would he eat? How did he do it? I later got the whole story.

Ralph had waited as planned until the corn was high. He knew the train times, how slow they ran going into the hill, and how fast he must run to latch onto one. Ralph and I many times that summer went through the cornfield to the railroads edge and when a train came by, he would race with it to see if he could keep up. He could almost outrun it by the time the tassels were on the corn. All Ralph had waited for was the time he thought was right for him. He knew what awaited him if he failed. Ralph had been awake about an hour before the first sunlight and had been building himself up to make the run. Ralph dressed without awaking anyone and slowly walked along the edge of the hall next to the wall. This prevented any creaks from the weak places in the floor.

He carried with him $8.00 cash in a small brown pouch (The money saved when kids' mothers came out on Sundays). Instead of turning the money over to Mrs. Barton we gave it to Ralph. Dimes and quarters. He also had no shoes, since every summer our shoes were worn out so that we all went barefoot. We enjoyed going barefoot and by midsummer our feet were like leather. Ralph was traveling light and for speed. As Ralph left the building he headed straight for the cornfield. He had to make the edge before the big boys woke up.

SILENT TEARS

Ralph waited about ten to fifteen minutes until a slow northbound train came, heading straight toward Nashville. As he sprang from the cornfield he ran as fast as his legs could carry him. Ralph grabbed a car ladder and got between two coal cars. They were empty. What an air of excitement and jubilation it must have been at that moment. Freedom at last. Ralph didn't even think about Nashville as he was noticing the green countryside float by. The large homes and pretty farms. The train was slowing down. It had come fifteen miles and was pulling into Radmar Yards, south of downtown Nashville. This was the main switching point for middle Tennessee and L and N Railroad. As the train came to a halt, Ralph waited at least two hours before he moved. He was unsure of what to do next. Finally, he looked out and saw no one in sight. He started walking north on the tracks until he left the yard. He came upon Thompson Lane. He pulled out his map and was looking it over when a small boy and girl about his age came up.

"What' cha doin'" asked the little girl.

Ralph, always the quick thinker, replied, "Just playing war games, it's for boys."

"Well, my brother is a boy, and we play war sometimes."

"I'm studying this map my cousin gave me, bet you don't know how to study maps," he said, still trying to shake the little girl and her brother.

The little girl, obviously a thinker herself, had an answer for that too. "We don't have to study maps; we always know where we are."

At that Ralph began to think that maybe a game or two of war might just be beneficial. "My name's Ralph, you can play with me if you want to."

"Mine's Cindy, and this is my brother, he's Robert," she said pointing to her smaller companion.

All introductions made, the three romped off to play until about noon, when the girl assured Ralph that her mom just loved to have other kids over for lunch.

When he entered their home, he knew the home he'd always hoped for was here. Cindy and Robert had a gracious mother, who did indeed like to have guests for lunch. Cindy explained that Ralph was visiting the neighborhood and her mother was glad to meet him, and didn't ask anything at all. After lunch Ralph and his new friends played until about five. He knew it was supper time by the smells around him. He told Cindy and Robert that he might see them the next day, and walked around until he found a little store to buy a loaf of bread and some bologna, a pint of milk, and cookies for dessert. As he ate, he sat down behind a store thinking about what he needed to do for the night. He went to Cindy's house after dark and slept in the bushes in their back yard. He knew where he was and that he could be safe there.

When morning woke him, Ralph went back to the store and ate another bologna sandwich, a few extra pieces of bread and threw the rest away. He knew he must find a more permanent home. A place out of the weather. It was getting dark and looked like rain. About noon the clouds opened up and Ralph was soaked to the bones. By this time, he had wandered about four miles further into Nashville coming upon the fair grounds. There were all kinds of buildings there and a few were leased out to farmers to hold livestock. It was in a lower income white neighborhood but it was clean and dry.

As Ralph came upon one building, he noticed boys about his age feeding livestock.

One of them saw Ralph and invited him to join in the fun. Ralph pitched in and in a few minutes, all was done. It was still raining outside. "Where are you from?" one interested boy asked.

"Franklin," answered Ralph, "I'm visiting my grandmother. Now the other kids were becoming more interested in Ralph and less interested in the livestock and began asking more questions. "Hey look" said the ever-cautious runaway, "it's stopped raining outside!"

They ran among the hay bales for about an hour and then his new friends had to leave and ralph just laid down to rest and rethink.

"Wake up punk," Ralph did, with a sharp punch to the ribs. You got any money on you?"

Over Ralph stood three men probably winos who roamed the area. The odor of alcohol was heavy, Ralph was dazed, and as one of the old men held him down, the others were going through his pockets. "Hey look! Coins." Ralph's fear probably saves him much pain, for he couldn't have moved a muscle if he had tried. This new and unexpected danger was more frightening than anything Ralph could have ever dreamt.

"Stay there, kid, and don't move at all, or we'll cut you to pieces." Just as they got to the edge of the barn, the kids Ralph had helped to feed the cows returned with the police. They had come back to play when they noticed the three men walk into the barn and surround Ralph. The fairgrounds were close to a Nashville sub-station and the boys had run to get help.

SILENT TEARS

They got my money," Ralph yelled. "And that skinny one had a knife."

What's your name, son?" asked one of the policemen.

Ralph was for once off guard and too scared to think. "Ralph," he said. "Ralph McCarty."

McCarty," one of the officers said. "I've heard that name somewhere."

Ralph couldn't believe himself; with all his careful planning and forethought, he'd made a terrible error. Trying to recoup, he pointed to the closest house and said, "My grandmother lives over there."

Well, you'd better go and get her and meet us at the substation," the officer said.

Ralph and the kids ran off. "I'm Jimmy and this is Timmy, my brother. You ran away from home, didn't you?"

"How did you know?" Ralph questioned.

"That was our house you pointed to!"

Ralph told Jimmy and Timmy about the orphanage and how things were, and about Mrs. Barton. They decided to help all they could. So, they made a deal for Ralph to stay in the barn and they would bring him food when they could. They all promised not to tell and they made a pact. Ralph remained this way for two more days. He roamed the fairgrounds with his new found friends. They even snuck Ralph home and let him take bathes while their mother was at work. This lasted for four more days, and finally the police picked Ralph up at the barn and learned from Jimmy and Timmy where he had come from.

SILENT TEARS

The Nashville newspaper carried a story about how Ralph was clothed and fed. How he came close to meeting a quick death and how any run-away might fair if they didn't meet good friends. Ralph was placed in a foster home for two days while investigations took place to confirm his confinement in the orphanage home. Ralph's story to the welfare workers of the brutality at the orphanage was put off as a wild tale. Nobody could believe this could take place at an orphanage home, especially at a Baptist orphanage home, without it being noticed at once. The paper stated Ralph would be brought back that Sunday. On Friday before that Sunday Mrs. Barton read us the newspaper account and said it doesn't pay to run away and place our lives in danger with crooks and thieves.

I guess her intention was to scare us more. It did me as I could see giants attacking Ralph. I slept very uneasy that night. All day Saturday it rained and as we stayed in the basement the rumors and conversation were all about Ralph. How close he came to death. How he got his name in the paper. The new clothes welfare gave him. Just everything a kid our age could think of. We knew Sunday would be a very exciting day.

FALL + WINTER 1950

After a week in Nashville and under a doctor's observation Ralph McCarty was returned to the orphanage. The first part of the day was spent at the school building and in Dr. Christain's office. Ralph and the welfare officer who returned him asked Dr. Christain to listen to the tales Ralph had to tell. After four hours Dr. Christain, the assistant superintendent Dr. Nolan and the secretary brought Ralph to the little boys building. We had just finished lunch and could see the small strange group approaching our building. Mrs. Barton was sitting near her flower garden and had no worry about the approaching storm. Dr. Christain told Ralph to go play while they had a conference with Mrs. Barton. We got our own group together and all the boys in our building huddled together to listen for hours on end of Ralph's adventures in Nashville. Little did we notice the breakup of Mrs. Barton's group after about two hours. She sat as still as a stone in a pond. She did not move until about supper time as we did not move either. We listened to Ralph rave on until the supper bell rang. Everybody was in a high. Ralph put fire into us and if he said at that moment we should throw Mrs. Barton out of the building, a revolt would have taken place. Mrs. Barton had not a word to say to anyone except wash up, form a line, and march to the cafeteria. After supper she lingered back talking to the matron of the little girls building. Mrs. Gimble was Mrs. Barton's age and once I had an occasion to be in the little girls building when she was whipping. She did not seem as harsh as Mrs. Barton, but was heavy with the belt, nevertheless. Her system of whipping was not constant. Between the two buildings is a park type area about seventy-five feet. We sat there and talked some more with Ralph. That was all we could think of. A rock road ran in back of our building and I don't remember who threw the first rock, but a sudden crash of a window pane in the little girls building went out. I looked up toward the building. I could see a second-floor window out. A spontaneous action and all of us were throwing rocks at the both buildings. A small riot had broken out. Our group was surrounded by matrons and bigger boys, but we pelted them or who ever came near us. This lasted a good thirty minutes. We were in control and knew the ending but held out until Dr. Christain walked among us.

Every boy from six on up had a rock in his hand. If anyone else tried to approach they were quickly rocked off. Dr Christain told everyone to leave the area, because he wanted to talk to us. He was Jesus to us. Always interested and concerned but there just wasn't enough of him to go around for all the children. He found a chair and we talked right there. All the children gathered around his chair and some broke down into tears as they told of everything that they could. We all were desperate to spill our hearts out to someone. We talked into the night. We needed someone to show us love and understanding. We told him how Mrs. Barton on Wednesday night made all of us undress and stand in line naked as we waited to take a shower. How she stared at us. The whippings, the standing on one foot until every muscle in our body ached… How she slapped us and how frightened we were of her. About ten o'clock that night we were exhausted. Dr. Christain saw us all to bed and stayed into the middle of the night talking to Mrs. Barton. We never knew what was said or what action was taken against us for the riot, but I knew, Gerald knew, and Ralph knew, we had had our moment. It was a very satisfying moment and most of us slept the most relaxed we had ever. The next morning everything was still exciting and it went until about ten that morning as routine things had to be done. Gerald was the first to notice Ralph was not with us or the other boys. Mrs. Barton had sent Bill Smotherman to the cafeteria for a tray lunch for Ralph who was sick and weak.

She spoke in a pleasant voice, which was one of the few times it was ever heard. It seemed normal since this was a happening about a tray lunch for whoever was sick. We were always made to stay in bed for any sign of sickness. Sometimes for two or three days with a fever. After Bill delivered the tray and returned, we asked Bill how Ralph was doing. We all thought he got sick in Nashville and brought it back with him. He did seem normal the night before though.

"I don't know, I didn't see him. Mrs. Barton has him in the sick room."

I told Gerald I sure would like to talk to Ralph some more about Nashville. "Well maybe when Mrs. Barton goes to the little girls building and visits with Mrs. Gimble today, we can sneak into the sick room and see him," replied Gerald.

About eleven o'clock Mrs. Barton finally went to the other building. "Come on, Tommy. Hurry! We won't have much time."

We ran into the building and up the stairs.

"Go on Tommy, and I'll stand guard for you." I raced up the last flight of stairs and rushed into the sick room. In the far corner next to the wall lay Ralph. His back was to me. I had brought him my new sling shot or flipper as we called it, Gerald had made it for me and it was the best I could do for a get well present.

SILENT TEARS

I THOUGHT Ralph was sleeping so I walked to the bed and laid my hand on his shoulder. He moved but did not turn toward me." Come on, Ralph. It's me, Tommy."

He could hardly move, but when he did turn over, I saw a person I could not believe was Ralph. Both his eyes were swollen together, his whole face was puffy, his arms were swollen and twice their normal size. He had cuts on his forehead and whelp marks on his arms and neck. I went to my knees and almost passed out with fright. I broke out crying, tears ran as never before and Ralph reached out to touch me and assure me to not wait but leave. He could hardly talk and his lips were cracked and bleeding.

"Leave Tommy, come back late tonight or some other time. Leave before you get caught."

About that time Gerald yelled," Come on Tommy, she is coming back" I just got downstairs and to the basement bathroom as Mrs. Barton walked in… I was still crying and throwing up.

"What are you two doing down there?" she yelled.

Gerald, the quick thinker, said, "Tommy is sick and throwing up. I brought him in."

"Well, if he's not better by lunch, we'll send him to bed."

I knew I could not go to bed, I had to tell Gerald what I saw. I got better but at lunch I could not eat. I hid my biscuits and cookies and knew Ralph was not being fed. Gerald saw me culling my cookies and did the same, as sneaking cookies for a snack was the thing to do. After lunch we went to the back yard. Gerald was wanting to hear what I saw and what had made me sick. For the afternoon we talked. Later Gerald snuck into the building and took Ralph a mason jar of water and the cookies. As he returned down the stairs Mrs. Barton had been down in the basement and was coming up again. To make Mrs. Barton think he just came in. Gerald turned around and started walking back up the stairs.

"Uh huh, sneaking in to see Ralph. Well, no one is to see him, and I'll make a lesson of you."

She gave Gerald six licks and made him stand in the hall outside her door for two hours. During this period of time the urge to ring the bell went through his mind but Gerald knew he had already gotten away with more than he should have and was pleased to stand out his time.

Ralph finally was allowed out of the sick room. His swelling had gone down and only a few bruises were left on his arms. It was getting close to school time again and unknown to us children (who knew not of the words child abuse or psychotic) and this was Mrs. Barton's problem. After the incident with Ralph, she must have been greatly relieved. The next few months her behavior was almost human. Not so many whippings, less yelling and every one in a while a smile. This was strange for us to handle and we of course lowered our guard.

Ralph seemed to be passive. He didn't talk of running away anymore and seemed to adjust to let things go.

I was now in the second grade. Gerald in the fourth, and Donald in the first.

As winter came, we were again looking forward to the Christmas before us. This period seemed the closest thing to a pure fantasy as I have ever known.

We could always tell when it was going to snow. The weather was not a freezing cold. The wind did not blow and the sky was covered with dull gray clouds. You could feel it. One night it snowed about ten inches. Since our school was in the orphanage we walked to school during any weather. Just to walked through the snow and hear the quietness of our footsteps, not a loud noise, just a soft squeeze was a pleasure one never forgets.

That night Bill Smotherman asked if anyone wanted an ice cycle. Of course, everyone in the room wanted one, ten kids. Bill stuffed pillows under his cover. He then opened up a window next to the fire escape. All he had on was pajamas and socks. As he went through the window he yelled, "and to all a good night" and he disappeared upward toward the roof. Bill had been gone about ten minutes when Mrs. Barton came into the room and yelled, for us to hush. "Who left this window opened? Now leave it shut and locked." With this she slammed the window shut and locked it. She stayed in the room about five minutes maybe hoping to see what or who might do something.

I was hoping Bill would not come down from the roof but I also knew he must be freezing.

After Mrs. Barton left the room Douglas Meyers quickly unlocked the window and looked toward the roof, no Bill. Douglas whispered to all "he's not there!" "Maybe he fell" If he did it would be a thirty-foot drop into a ten-inch-deep snow. We all looked toward the ground but saw nothing. Five more minutes went by as we laid in bed thinking where was Bill? A knock at the window brought us all up in bed. At the window was a big figure of a kid with both arms wrapped in about ten of the biggest ice-cycles I had ever seen. We all took one and never told Bill about Mrs. Barton. We all sounded like puppies licking water from a creek. Slurp, slurp, slurp. Boy were they good and cold, and boy were they big!

SILENT TEARS

After we finished Bill told us to guess what he saw on the roof. To our amazement we expected anything and that was just what Bill reeled off. "I saw Mrs. Barton smoking when I first went out and was by her window getting ice-cycles. I saw her smoking a cigarette. I saw her leave the room then I kept on getting ice cycles." Boy, were we stunned. Smoking was a sin in a Baptist school. We could hardly wait until the next day to start all kinds of rumors. This finally died off like all rumors and the old routine returned. This winter was to be a rough winter. I turned eight in January and the year was 1950. We now had been at the orphanage for three years.

SAVED IN THE WINTER

1950 was remembered in the Southwest and Southeast as the year of the blizzard. It snowed and ice covered the entire area. Electricity was out at the orphanage and soon our heat went. Mrs. Barton issued extra blankets to each kid. We slept in our clothes. At night we crawled into our beds until our body built up a heated area then slowly, we stretched out until asleep. In the mornings Mrs. Barton had two boys to tale a bucket and get coal from the furnace house… The furnace house supplied all heat through radiators. All coal had run out and only enough for fireplaces was left. After the boys brought the coal back Mrs. Barton unbanked her fire and heated her room up. Then we were marched into her room in threes and fours and stood by the fireplace. Each group had about two minutes to warm up as this would be the only real heat to reach our bodies all day. For food, sandwiches were brought over usually they were one meat and one apple butter. Donald and I ate our two up and hour later Gerald would come over and divide his apple butter and give each a half Gerald watched over us as if were his own kids. He would hussle us together with his arms around us telling of how it will be when we could leave. The cold went on for about three weeks without heat or electricity. For water we ate snow and sucked in ice cycles. To everybody's amazement no one got sick. Mrs. Barton never came from her room except during lunch and bedtime to us it was just as well.

Finally, the electricity came on and two weeks later a coal truck came then and again we had heat. With this we were allowed to return to school.

As things returned to normal in school new talk of being baptized aroused in class. It seemed we always had church and even in school. As a kid I believed anything about God as the truth. I just wondered how come he never answer my prayers and left us in the orphanage.

I remember Douglas Meyers and Raymond Aldridge talking about how their folks said you got a burning sensation in your heart. Boy I bet that hurt. Raymond said you could get a trip to Nashville and at night if you got baptized. The wheels started turning in my head a trip. I got all the information on how to act Christian and started on my way for the trip. That Sunday the fourth in each month. Dr. Christian asked people to become Christian. That was my cue. I walked up to shake his hand and told him I was a Christian. I believed in God and I had a burning sensation in my heart. I was seated with about six other boys from my class, and about fifteen all together. After church services I was told that next Sunday at five pm we would travel to Nashville to the First Baptist Church and be Baptized. My trip at last.

That Sunday after church and after lunch Mrs. Barton made all six of us to be baptized come and lay down. She walked into the room and said she was proud of us. She also said that after being baptized we could not lie anymore and if we did, we would go to hell. None of us slept as the trip away from her was what we were really looking forward to. About five she told us to get dressed. We wore white socks and a white dress shirt. These were special clothes kept in a room in the attic.

One of the other teachers drove us to Nashville and we were excited as could be. We came upon a big church old red brick type. The streets were really crowded. Life was moving here. People were everywhere. At the church we were led to the first row and sat through a long service. Then came the time. I knew I had lied about God. He never talked to me and besides my heart was not on fire. We walked into a small dressing room. I remember one man well who was to be baptized from this church. He was about six feet tall, heavy for his age and stuck something up his nose and sniffed. "Aw, that's better" he said and laid it down. I picked it up and stuck it to my nose. I jerked my head back as the menthol entered. Gosh I thought he must be crazy for doing that.

I watched from the side as people walked out into the water and from the side that was all I could see. When my turn came, I entered into the water. It was like a big tub. The water was warm. I kept my eye on the preacher until I was by his side. I then noticed the people in the audience. There were a lot of people there. About that time and without warning I was under water. I came up chocking and gagging and stumbled into the back room… Was that quick. I felt no different except being a little wet. I asked Bobby Brewer if he felt any different and he said no but he had peed in the water I remember he went before me.

Spring or Summer 1950

The Runt

Among my friends was a boy named John Nay. John had an older brother William. They kept a low profile not upsetting anyone. Since they were about a year apart in age and big for their age, nobody picked on them. It became known in a hurry if you fought one you fought the other. These two were not from the Nashville area and it seemed God had more to moving them than other kids. Leave them alone and they left you alone. John would chase butterflies and put stingers out of honeybees. He would hold the bee by its wing then remove its stinger. He showed me that if you pull the bee apart a small bag of honey was inside the rear pouch.

John would have in later years been called a flower child. John had a lot of odd ball ways and it seemed to keep him or someone in trouble. William was an athlete. He played baseball and basketball. William read a lot and he and Gerald were together talking about books sometimes all day.

One day after school John approached me and asked if I would like to meet Checkers.

"Who's Checkers," I asked.

"Oh, just something I've found. Interested?"

"Yes," I replied and John led me past the swing set in the back yard near an old Elm tree. Inside were small field mice, about half grown. In this group was a gray with black spots runt.

"Boy, he's small, what are you going to do with him?"

"Well tonight I'm going to take him in and make him a home." And John picked up the small mouse and placed it in his shirt pocket. It did not move as the heat from John's body gave it a sense of being and warmth. As supper time approached, I asked John what about the mouse.

"I'll keep him in my pocket until after supper and then make him a house. At supper I'll slip him some crumbs into my pocket and feed him."

"What if he moves?" I asked, worried.

"Well, it's a big shirt and the pockets are heavy, if he moves it'll be hard to see."

That night at the supper table John sat at one end and I sat across from him Mrs. Barton was at the head of the table and one older girl who brought food sat at the other end. The inside of the cafeteria was big. It seated about one hundred and fifty people from the three buildings at once and there were no bugs, rats, or anything except humans alive in our buildings. They did keep down the bugs and rats.

As we were about to finish our supper, I noticed John's mouse poke it's head from his pocket. I couldn't say anything and the other boys at our table didn't know John had a mouse. As I tried to poke other boys to tell John, they thought John was pulling a prank by bringing in the mouse. John was still unaware of his mouse slipping out of his pocket.

SILENT TEARS

John's pocket top was level with the table and the mouse crawled out onto the table. The table was about twenty feet long and sat ten boys, Mrs. Barton and the girls. As the mouse moved down the table checking plates, giggles came from everybody. On one let on what was happening and knew what would happen if Mrs. Barton looked up. Here came the girl with a new tray of cream potatoes and as she was sitting down, they tray a piercing scream (which froze John and anyone else who didn't at first see the mouse) came from her lips. John was covered with cream potatoes and every boy at our table broke into uncontrollable laughter. The mouse took the shortest unobstructed path, toward Mrs. Barton.

She had nowhere to go and Mrs. Barton's mouth open and she turned white and went out like a light. By this time the mouse was being wacked at with spoons and knives and it became an instant relief to let off steam in the form of chasing the mouse. Bill Smotherman picked up the mouse and passed it to the next table to let them have a try at it. Pandemonium was rampant for about fifteen minutes. It was hard to believe that that mouse got away after looking at the tables and broken dishes.

The other matrons took Mrs. Barton outside and walked her around until she regained her senses. By this time everyone was outside and wondering where the mouse came from.

I found John and the first words were of concern for his checkers. After a conversation of about ten minutes, we returned to the little boys building and John knew Mrs. Barton would be late returning, so he headed for the dead elm tree. He returned a few minutes later and had the rest of the small mice in his pocket.

"Don't tell anybody. I'm going to put these into Mrs. Barton's bed."

SILENT TEARS

There have been few times when I was scared to death and thinking about what would happen if she found out was one. We discussed among ourselves, John, Ralph, Bill Smotherman, Gerald and myself. It was decided no matter what or who God was to lie, lie, lie, when it happened. Ralph and John made the run to her room and Bill stood guard. In a short time, Ralph and John returned and we made an oath not to pass the word to anyone else for fear of Mrs. Barton finding out.

Here she came still a little jumpy and nervous and starting sending everyone to bed. She made her rounds to every room and the few of us who knew of the mice waited for the scream to come from her room.

It was about thirty minutes. Maybe they crawled out of the bed or maybe she had a cigarette before she uncovered them. But when she found them the whole building shook from her scream. A loud thump was heard and dead silence. The few who knew let on like they didn't. A few of the older boys were brave enough to approach and know. No answer. Jessie Steward knocked hard. "Mrs. Barton, are you in there?" No answer. "Maybe someone killed her!" The feeling of those few words sent chills up everybody's spine. "Maybe they are still in there," someone yelled, and you could see the impending panic. "Yeah, I can hear someone moving" "They're coming after us!" Ralph yelled; the race was on.

Everyone fled from the building yelling to the top of their lungs, Ralph! Bill walked over slowly and opened her door. Looking in we saw Mrs. Barton stretched out on the floor breathing but out like a light. Gerald closed the door and said we should act like everyone else and flee the building. We did, screaming as if the devil were after us.

SILENT TEARS

A few of the older boys were there by now so tales of a killer were floating in the air.

That night Mrs. Barton was put in the hospital for rest and an older boy stayed with us. No one ever knew what really happened except John, Ralph, Bill, Gerald, and me, and of course Mrs. Barton, and she must have wondered, because before we left Bill, Ralph, and John rounded up the mice and put them back in the old dead elm.

Summer 1950

William Nay Drowns

The rest of March 1950 through May 1950 went as time spent in limbo. No real happenings, or events took place. The Korean War was making headlines and a few older boys were leaving and going into the army.

Mother would come to see us more often and every once in a while, she would give us a few coins to buy candy at the Texaco store. Of course, we had to send a bigger boy or sneak up there ourselves. Mrs. Barton had taken money from me she said to keep in the form of a half dollar, a nickel, a dime. and two pennies. Every time she took it, I engraved it into my sub conscious the amounts and when, so I'd never forget. At last summer was upon us and the pond on the south side of the orphan age was used as a swimming hole.

We were allowed to swim under supervision of a new young and very pretty secretary to Mr. Christian, Julie Medows. Julie's duties were light during the summer and she acted as a sports counsellor and activity director. Julie was nineteen and very mature for her age.

William Nay, John's older brother, was about seventeen at this time, and had taken a special interest in Julie. William and John had no Father, mother, cousins aunts or uncles to their or anyone else's knowledge. They were the only people I have ever known to be completely alone.

William used Julie as a friend, mother, and sounding board. It seemed he was all alone and unsure about his future. He was receiving no formal training and the military was to be his only out. He worried about John and what would happen to him when he left, who would protect him the way William had.

Julie was very understanding and took the time to talk to William. She let him know her sincere interest in his problems and at times it seemed to relieve the pressures of living.

These talks continued on into the summer and Julie had a handle on the situation About the middle of summer Julie announced to the world that she was getting married. The marriage was to be performed at the orphanage and what excitement it created! I had never seen a wedding, only pictures.

As the wedding date approached, William and Julie had their talks on the banks of the pond as the other boys swam.

"Julie I am happy for you, really," William said.

" William, I know I will be happy, and maybe you and John can come and see us sometime, during holiday break. "

"I sure hope so." replied William.

Julie had noticed William's far away looks and had often wondered about all the thoughts deeper in his mind. She had worried over the lost and empty feelings Willian had told her about. Julie had mentioned to Dr. Christian the fear she had for William breaking down. She knew he needed professional help, more than she could give. There was no money and very little psychiatric help coming in at any time. No one could detect or prevent the problems of the residents at the home.

About a week before the wedding William and six of the older boys were cleaning rocks from around the pond.

Julie was reading a book and hardly noticed as William came up and sat down... "Hi, Julie." he started.

"Oh, hi, William," she said.

"You know Julie, I'll really miss you when you're married and gone. You have been the best friend I have ever had. I told John how much I enjoy being around you. You're the sweetest person I've ever met.

"Well, thank you, William. That's the nicest thing anyone ever said to me. I know that I'll miss you, too."

"I guess I'd better get back and help the guys finish around the pond. I'll talk to you later."

Julie smiled up at William and watched him walk away, and continued reading her book

The other boys were coming out as William was going in. Bobby Moon was now sixteen and built like an ox. " We're all finished up in there William, no need to get back in "

"I think I'll just get in and swim a minute, " William said.

"Suit yourself, " said Bobby, and left the pond. "Miss Medows, we're through" I guess we'll go in and get ready for supper. William is still in." said Bobby as he was leaving.

"Thanks Bobby, I think I'll get William out and be right in, too."

Bobby and the others had just closed the gate and Julie turned to find William in the pond. It wasn't a large pond, only six and a half foot deep at its deepest point. Most of it was about four foot deep. William surfaced and waved at Julie slowly. Julie waved back and yelled, "come on William, time to go!"

William waved back again and said, "good bye," as he was sinking into the water.

Julie was frozen in horror, as her worst fears were coming true. William sank beneath the water with his hand still raised until it, too was swallowed up. William was only in about four feet of water, but Julie could not move.

"William!" Julie screamed. Bobby turned and caught sight of her sinking to the ground on her knees.

"Let's go," said Moon to rest of the guys, and he leaped over the fence and started running for the pond. Bobby reached Julie and she was pointing to the spot where William had disappeared. She was unable to speak and locked in shock, so Moon tock over. "Go get Dr. Christian, Ned. Bill, go get more help. The rest follow me into the pond."

Bill Sweeny ran past me on his way to get help. "What's wrong, Bill?" I yelled.

"William Nay drowned in the pond!"

My knees started shaking. I couldn't believe what I heard. I looked around and saw the assistant superintendent was in the field plowing. I started running toward him yelling and waving my arms. He glanced up and saw the tears on my face.

"What's wrong?"

SILENT TEARS

"William Nay just drowned in the pond!"

Mr. Kaiser leaped from the tractor and ran faster than I could have believed a fifty-year-old man could.

I walked back to the yard and by than everyone had heard what had happened< Bobby Moon and the other two boys were walking the pond and Moon stepped on William. Without wasting a moment, he picked up William and walked to the edge of the pond. Julie was crying hysterically. Mr. Kaiser was giving artificial respiration. In about fifteen minutes and ambulance arrived, although William was still alive. He died on route to the hospital.

Summer 1950

The Funeral

The news of William's death was given front page in the Nashville newspapers The funeral was planned for the orphanage because of no living relatives except John survived. A stunned silence lay over the orphanage for the three days prior to the funeral.

During this period of grief many stories were told about William. His unselfishness with his time for others, the deeds of goodwill, his faith. His death was treated as a simple drowning and the help he should have received was all but gone. The vein efforts and pleadings of Miss Meadows got swallowed up in the events of the day.

I never saw a dead person before and now the anticipation of seeing William caused my body to tremble. I couldn't sleep and when I did, I had nightmares of seeing and playing with John and William, and their sub-conscious would awake me in a cold sweat. Death is man's main fear in life. This first contact death has haunted me to this day.

The funeral was to take place on Thursday at about 10:00 a.m. We all were dressed in the newest clothes we had. In silence we walked in line to the main auditorium of the school which also was a church. There were many strange people dressed in the latest fashions of the day sitting around the edge of the room, most were there out of courtesy and I noticed smiles on their faces as we were paraded before them. It had turned into a show of sorts.

Ralph brushed my arm and whispered, "I bet most of them have false teeth."

"Why?"

"Because they all grin alike."

Sure enough, I looked again and as if one monkey after another, they all looked exactly alike, strange. I had temporarily lost track of what was happening.

" Look at all those flowers," said Douglas, "ain't they pretty?"

"Can you see William?" asked Bill.

"No, they have him too deep inside,"

"Are you going to look at him?" asked Ralph.

"I guess, I never saw a real dead person." My heart quickened,

Dr. Christian began the sermon and a few songs followed. The casket was closed and I felt relieved that maybe we would not see him after all.

The casket was rolled down the north aisle right past me. A few tears followed as I felt sorry that he was to be placed in the ground.

We sat in our seats until the forward rows were emptied first and so on. I noticed the line took forever getting out, as I knew it never took this long before. As we were exiting the double doors, they had the casket opened and everyone was filing past in a single line. I heard loud crying and kids breaking down. I was getting weak as I approached the coffin, knowing it would be hard not to take a look... My head was about six inches over the top of the casket. I could see the face all white and so cold. looking. I walked past looking over the entire body, he had on a dark blue suit, white shirt, his hair parted on the right side. I almost fainted but Ralph held me up. He could take anything.

As Ralph was leading me out to the fresh air, one of the women (who I'm sure didn't know). William remarked that the children here seemed to be quite a lot of actors, that our grief was all a show. I felt Ralph's arm tighten up and knew he had also heard. I knew what would happen, and I tried to hold Ralph back, but to no avail.

Mrs. Barton also heard the woman's words and seemed to be offended, then she saw Ralph and knew that he was about to cause a scene. As Ralph approached the old woman, Mrs. Barton locked her eyes to his, as though she were just daring him to get out of line. Ralph stopped a few steps from the woman and spoke in a low soft voice," You sure remind me of my grandmother, you sure are pretty." Ralph seemed to be an angel; I could believe I heard this right.

The woman turned as though the blush, and immediately Ralph gave her a big hug. To my relief a confrontation had been avoided. After a few seconds the woman left in tears. What a touching moment. Everyone else witnessing could not believe that Ralph had finally mellowed. Mrs. Barton was gleaming with pride and was convinced Ralph had finally become something she had molded.

"Come on Tommy," said Ralph, "let's go wave to that woman."

"Ralph, do you have a grandmother?" I asked.

"No!"

"Well, how do you know she looked like that?"

"She doesn't."

SILENT TEARS

I stood stunned and with Ralph, waved good-bye to the woman. She was driving but crying so hard she could hardly see to steer as she left.

"I thought you were real mad at first," I said, trying to figure out how this had all turned around.

"I was and still am." Ralph said. "You just didn't hear everything I had to say to that old woman.

"But then, what did you say?" I asked.

"Don't ever tell."

"I won't, I promise."

"Well, I saw Mrs. Barton watching, and Brother Christian was near also. After the old woman hugged me, I grabbed her and while pretending to hug her, I told her, 'You old bitch, haul your ass out of here now or I'll stomp the shit out of you.' And I had a good grip on her neck the whole time."

My mouth fell open to the ground. These were the worst cuss words I had ever heard used in a sentence and was completely lost for words. As we walked toward our building the once passive Ralph remarked, "And I'm also going to run away again!"

At last, I understood, Ralph had never changed at all, he had just gotten sneaky.

1951

The Powers that Be

I now was about to enter the second grade. My ranking in power was on the upper end, but still a few older boys lined up the newer ones for beatings. I was now in the position Gerald had been when I first moved to the Little Boys Building. Donald was here with me, and smaller. Gerald was moved to the Big Boys Building and the pressures there were completely different. There was no power structure. They were mature and had little time for petty fights. Everyone in the Big Boys Building had to work for the home, to keep it functioning.

The first few months of school were calm and easy. But with the onset of winter and longer periods of confinement to the basement, tempers started clashing, and conflicts erupted to the surface. With little else to do the bigger boys started using the time to exercise their authority and power.

In the basement every boy had a box for his personal possessions. They were kept lined on a low wall which went all around the room. About the easiest way to get into big trouble was to get caught digging into someone else's box. It was against our rules and our moral principles to get into another boy's "territory".

The plumbing was exposed in the basement, a foot or two below the ceiling. We would jump on the pipes and go tomwalking around the rooms, like monkeys in a zoo. This is how Donald and about six other boys entertained themselves one day, when they were kept in from school for coughing and sneezing. While they were tomwalking a pipe began to leak, and the boxes started to get wet. They moved the boxes and went to find someone so they could report the leak. The pipe was fixed right away, but the young boys didn't think about putting the boxes back where they belonged.

That evening when the rest of the boys got in from school and found their boxes had been moved, they became furious. Immediately a guard was placed by the door, and all the kids who had stayed in from school that day were lined up in a corner. Panic set over me when I saw Donald standing in that group, trembling. I couldn't do a thing; else I'd be beat too. Ralph and I were not beat anymore because we were bigger and besides, Ralph always fought back. No matter what anyone did, Ralph kept coming back. If he couldn't get them back awake, he come in the middle of the night and none of them wanted to experience that pain more than once.

I was scared. "Ralph, what am I going to do?" I asked. " Jo Bob Miller is really mad. He's going to beat them bad!"

"You go start picking on them, I'll be back in a second."

"They'll tear me to pieces!"

"Naw, they won't have time. I can sneak to my box without being seen if you'll pick on them for a minute."

I didn't know what kind of crazy plan Ralph had, and I didn't know how to pick on one of the biggest boys in the building. Ralph started going through the crowd of the rest of the boys, whispering to them. Some went to their boxes, and Ralph went to his. I didn't know what was on Ralph's mind, But I always had the feeling that I could trust him.

I stood opposite of Jo Bob and about three yards away. I gave myself plenty of running room in case fists started flying. Before I knew it, they were moving in on the little guys. "Hey, Jo Bob!"

" What's your problem?" Jo Bob said, turning toward me.

I took a small step back. "You're not going to beat Donald up, " I stuttered, and swallowed hard. I thought I must be crazy. I was asking for the worst beating of my life, I didn't know what to say next. Jo Bob was leering at me.

About then I felt Ralph at my side. I was shaking and fear was evident on my face. couldn't move, I was scared. I felt Ralph grab my hand, I looked down. He was putting a stick in my hand. I withered.

Ralph was like a stone wall. His vocabulary had improved to greater limits as he started barking out commands. "From now on, no more beatings! Anyone who beats up these smaller kids for the hell of it answers to me!"

My shoulders started squaring. What power! I felt like I could take on the world (with Ralph at my side). I glanced around" and About ten other kids had clubs. Ralph had built an army of these guys like me, finished with our brutalization, but tired of seeing the smaller ones picked on.

Ralph walked through Jo Bob and his gang. They were shocked of this challenge to their authority. Ralph reached into his box and brought out an orange. He placed it on the middle table. Everybody's eyes were glued to the orange. "Look at it," he said. Not a word was spoken and for a few tense moments all eyes were glued to the orange. WHAM!!!!!! What a shattering blow Ralph made as he brought his club down on the orange. Juice splattered everywhere. It scared me to death. Ralph had their attention.

"Just pretend that's your head," he said, pointing to the flattened orange. "Maybe I can be whipped, but I'll get you back while you sleep. So, whoever wants to lay a hand on them goes round with me first, right now." he raised the stick in his hand a little higher.

The challenge was made. Jo Bob had to meet it or forfeit power. He just walked away. I know he must have thought Ralph was nuts. From then on no one tried to beat the littler guys just because they were mad. Ralph had had his day. I noticed my pants were wet.

MARCH 1951

MRS. BARTON'S VACATION

This year, my third-grade year, seemed shortened compared to most. Mrs. Barton all of a sudden left for Nashville for about a month. The story was that she was ill.

For the month of March, an older girl from the Jarmon Building was our overseer. Her name was Janice Mays, and she was about seventeen or eighteen. At night Josh Peterman came over to help put us to bed. Josh was kind and gentle. He was Janice's age and they had eyes for each other, and as everything worked out, all the boys in the building just thought of the m like mother and father.

During the mornings Janice helped us make the beds and praised us for jobs well done. Josh came over in the evenings to help get our baths, and told us stories. For this month we were allowed to be children again and let our defensive shields down.

We all got along together better without Mrs. Barton's threatening presence.

Up to now Unise Dean was the most we knew about sex. We had girlfriends in school, and talked like all boys do, trying to sort out the truth about such matters among ourselves. Josh and Janice sorted out the truth for all of us one night in March.

Bill Smotherman was out on one of his roof walks, and came back in a rush, very excited. "Boy, try to Guess what I saw!" His voice was high and generated excitement.

"What?" asked Ralph.

"Josh and Janice don't have any clothes on, and they're in bed together!"

"None?"

"No, none! Come on!"

Everyone was eager to see and it seemed like the whole floor was on the fire escape at once. About ten of us were on the roof, and what an education we had. I didn't know a man could do all those things. We were all squirming and I'm sure none of us really understood why we were affected by this the way we were. After a few minutes we were too cold to watch any more. As we were leaving, Mr. Bailey the headmaster over the big boys building was coming to our building with his wife. "I wonder what's taking Josh so long?" he asked his wife.

"Well, we were young once. It's not always easy to leave a pretty girl." she replied.

At once we knew Josh could not be caught this way. We decided he would have to know we were watching to save his skin. "Ya'll go knock, and tell Josh to come out the window, I'll wait here and show him how to get around." said Bill.

We scampered into the window and knocked on the door. "Josh, Mr. Bailey is coming. Go out the window."

Josh was out the window and grabbing his clothes without a moment's hesitation. Bill was smiling like the Cheshire cat." You kids been out here watching?" Josh asked.

"Yep" replied Bill," you better come on, or we'll both get skinned. Josh stumbled across the roof stark naked. Josh and Bill were entering the attic when Mr. and Mrs. Bailey were at Janice's door. Janice answered and said, "Josh was telling the kids some stories, but I got sleepy and came on to bed."

"Josh!" Mr. Bailey yelled up the stairs.

"Up here, Mr. Bailey, In the attic."

Josh finished dressing as Mr. Bailey was coming up the stairs. "We got worried Josh, and it's time for these boys to be in bed." said Mr. Bailey.

"Right Mr. Bailey, I'll come right on over." said Josh.

"Okay, and hurry. 'Night, boys!"

" Good night, Mr. Bailey!" we all answered.

Josh caught his breath and started laughing. "You son of a guns! Thanks." and he left, still laughing. He stopped by Janice's door and said good-night to her again, and they both started laughing. They probably laugh about that still. Four years later Josh came back from Korean war and married Janice.

Mrs. Barton came back from Nashville a different person. She had softened up, and after that she didn't whip kids as often or as hard. Her attitude was changing and she seemed a little gentler.

I am now nine years old.

SILENT TEARS

April or May 1951

The Band

The only activity which included travel besides being baptized was the band. The church provided a few instruments and getting in the band was limited to a few talented kids. A few parents provided an instrument. Gerald and I were lucky in that our aunts wanted to help out as much as mother would allow. Aunt Edna bought me a saxophone and Gerald got a trumpet from Aunt Clara. How proud I was of my sax. It came in a black case with red velvet and was silver. It took much of my time just to learn to read music, much less put sound to it. After a few months I was able to play a few notes. What I didn't understand I just faked. Gerald, though, was very talented and could read as well as play. Gerald moved up to first trumpet in a few months. We were together a lot this way.

Just before school was out the First Baptist Church in Nashville sent a bus for the band. We were to leave that afternoon and return later that night. Our leader would not be on this trip with us. Everyone in the band was given one dollar to put in the plate when it was passed in church.

Just to hold a dollar and put it in my pocket and carry it around for a few hours was a pleasure. I never had that much money before.

We arrived in Nashville and went directly to the church to unload our instruments. A small lunch was served and the church had planned a short tour of Nashville for us before church began. This was a bigger thrill than I had expected.

The band was assembled at the side of the church, waiting for a bus to go to the State Capitol Building. In the bus lane next to the church many buses passed with different headings. One bus with Porter Road stopped next to us, and without hesitating Gerald said, "Come on!". Gerald, Bobby Moon Rivers, and I jumped on the bus, pulling out our dollars, and getting back eighty-five cents change.

"This bus circles Nashville," explained Gerald.

"I don't care where it goes," said Bobby, "just don't get us lost."

Gerald's memory was good. When we came home with Mother during the summer for two weeks, we went everywhere on the city bus. Gerald knew what he was doing. The bus circled Nashville. About a half mile from the church, we got off to walk. We on were foot loose and had money in our pockets. On 5th avenue and the arcade, we bought a bag of popcorn for ten cents and a coke for five cents and still had money in our pockets.

As we were walking past an alley, Bobby grabbed Gerald's arm and said, "Look!".

In the alley on a four-wheel platform was a man without any legs. He had two blocks to move himself with but at the moment was drunk with a wine bottle in his arms. I was stunned and sickened. All I could think of was how he slept, how did he dress, how did he make money? I could have cried. I followed the other guys over and squatted to talk to him. Bobby Moon started asking the questions I had been thinking and I was sure we all had been thinking. The old man brightened up at the attention and answered anything we asked. He had lost his legs during W.W. II. He never married, but he did have a brother in Nashville. He received a government pension but could afford very little. He said he begged most of the time. He asked us where we were from.

SILENT TEARS

"The Baptist Orphanage Home," explained Rivers.

"Well," He said, "you better get going. It's getting dark soon, and an alley is not a safe place to be after dark."

We all smiled half-heartedly and started moving toward the street. "How much money have y'all got?" Moon asked us.

We all had 65 cents and we all were thinking along the same lines, so as Bobby held out his hand, we all emptied our pockets into it. He ran back to the old ran and put the money into it, and ran back to join us. We all felt much better, although dead broke.

We waited in the doorway by the church until the tour bus pulled up, and just fell in with the rest of the guys when they were unloading. If anyone noticed we hadn't been along on the tour, they never said anything.

Inside the church we were all given envelops and told to put our dollar into it, and to put it in the plate when it was passed.

"What are we going to do, Gerald?" I asked. "All our money's gone."

"Just look at it like this," said Gerald, "the church takes this money to help the poor, and we just did it ourselves."

"But what if someone sees us?"

"Just put a piece of paper in the envelop and it will look like your dollar is in there."

This still did not sooth my conscious. "But God will be watching."

SILENT TEARS

"Don't get upset, Tommy, we don't do that much wrong. Why don't you just write God a note and put it in there, He will understand."

I sat there and thought about what to write to God. "Bless the man with no legs," I wrote. " Keep him warm, give him food." I hoped God would understand. I was very depressed.

When I was a sophomore in High School years later, I thought about the old man again when I saw a sign in a store window which read, "I complained because I had no shoes, until I met a man who had no feet."

THE BIGGEST WATERMELON

Before the summer of '51 was over, rumors had reached our building of the biggest watermelon ever being at the grocery store on Franklin Road. Several of the older boys told us stories of the watermelon so big it must have taken six men to set it on the table.

Gary Richardson had an idea. "Let's send someone up there and find out how much it costs. If we can, let's get all our monies together and buy it and have one last feast with parched corn in the corn field."

This was the greatest thing to happen since Ralph had run off. This was something to look forward to just before school started.

Well as things went, Ralph was the only kid with nerve to sneak up to the store. Just before supper, he faked sick and Mrs. Barton sent him to bed. The store closed at 7:00 and supper was at 5:00.

We marched to supper that night and couldn't wait to hear Ralph's story later. After our building emptied for the cafeteria Ralph leaped out of bed and headed for the store. As he entered through the front door, his first question was, "Where is it?"

The store keeper knew what he meant and pointed to the watermelon. Many had been in to the store, and all wanted to see the melon. Ralph's eyes almost popped out; he couldn't believe what he was seeing. The melon was as big in weight and half his height. It weighed at least 80 pounds.

"Where did it come from?"

"I grew it," replied the storekeeper, with pride.

"How much do you want for it?"

"Sonny, I don't think you can afford it."

"How much?"

"Twenty dollars."

"I'll be back. "

With that Ralph left, but could think of nothing else but that melon. Whether or not twenty dollars existed in our group, the challenge was out. The next day, teams of threes set out to collect all they could. It's surprising how much money had been rat-holed from Mrs. Barton. Douglas and Bill Meyers had five dollars between them. I had fifteen cents, and so it went all day. After all the dimes and nickels were counted, we had eighteen dollars and seventy-three cents. Some of the kids had brothers or sisters in the other buildings, and with them, twenty dollars was finally collected.

Now came our greatest obstacle, getting the watermelon to the cornfield. The store was a half mile as a crow flies, and moving an eighty-pound melon presented a real challenge. Ralph and Bill Smotherman were the two strongest guys in our building. Bill had few brains, but was strong as an ox.

As the sun rose that Saturday morning the Odyssey of heavy moving began. Ralph and Bill both now were working on the laundry on Saturday. Their jobs consisted of getting all the clothes for our building to our basement and separating them. Gerald and I were to separate them while Bill and Ralph went after the, melon. With the help of an older boy all the clothes were brought to our

SILENT TEARS

building in one trip. On the second trip back to the laundry Mrs. Barton decided to visit Mrs. Bennigan in the Jarmon Building. The Jarmon Building faced the highway and of course Mrs. Bennigan had two chairs set up in the front facing the highway.

Ralph and Bill entered the store and were about to lay out the twenty dollars for the melon, when the storekeeper knew what problems, orphans had of obtaining twenty dollars.

"You kids really want that melon?"

"Sure, and we got twenty dollars in cash."

"Do you boys realize how much care and time it took to grow this melon?"

Ralph began to think it's going to take more than twenty dollars now. Bill stood amazed and said, "Years, huh?"

"Yeah, a long time. Now I'll feel bad taking all your money knowing how hard ya'll must have saved. Tell you what I'll do, I'll give it to you."

For a few seconds Ralph and Bill stood in stunned silence. "For real?" Ralph asked.

"Sure, son, for real?" said the storekeeper. "Just prove to me that you can move it, get it off the table, just you two, and move it."

Ralph and Bill went outside to ponder their problem. "Just think, Bill, we can have the melon and all our money too."

"Well, how are we going to move it?"

"Come here, Bill, " beckoned Ralph, leading Bill out behind the outhouse. Finding a loose plank, Ralph and Bill ripped the board free.

SILENT TEARS

As they walked back into the store, the storekeeper looked dumbfounded as the kids laid the plank next to the table and floor and started rolling the melon down. Down to the floor and out the door to the highway. "Bye, and thank-you!" said Ralph as the melon rolled past the storekeeper. It was hard to keep from laughing as his prize melon went rolling down the highway with two kids, not much larger hanging on and trying to control it.

"Clara, look at those kids on the highway!" said Mrs. Bennigan. The distance was greater than their eyesight could focus. "I don't believe those are our kids.

I know we don't have one as fat as the one up in front."

"I never saw a kid run so fast, and be that heavy, " replied Mrs. Barton.

"Bill, slow it down!"

"I can't get in front of it! You slow it down!"

The melon was on a downhill roll and picking up momentum.

"We're going to lose it. Watch out Bill, a truck!" Just as they jumped into a bar ditch, a semi smashed into the melon and splattered watermelon everywhere.

"Clara, Clara, the fat kid just got run over by a truck!" As Mrs. Bennigan turned around, Mrs. Barton was out, strung over her chair. The wreck was too much for her… Mrs. Bennigan started running to the highway, her yelling gained attention of others, and a crowd built up running to the highway behind her.

"Oh, no, Bill, stay low and run. Here comes trouble."

SILENT TEARS

Eyeing the crowd, bill needed no warning as both boys started in the bar ditch and headed for the cornfield.

Out of breath and panting, Bill and Ralph reached our group and we were glad to witnessed the roll.

"Well, I only lost fifteen cents."

No, you didn't, Tommy. I still have twenty dollars." Said Ralph, and in a fraction of the time it took to collect the money, it was redistributed. Bill explained what happened.

On the highway we could see the small crowd breaking up, and Mrs. Bennigan's embarrassment at being mistaken. As they walked back to the Jarmon Building, she was heard to mutter, "I wish those nigger kids would stay off the highway. Damn watermelon eaters, it's a wonder they're not back there, eating what's left.

1952 HOLIDAYS

In the fall of '51 the Korean War was at its height. I was now entering third grade, and Mother came more frequently on Sundays. With Mother came Carl Mason. Carl was a short stocky man. His curly black hair was full and a strong hard face showed many years of wear. His accent was noticeable with a strong northern Pennsylvania Dutch slang. His clothes fit to a tee. His walk showed the military in him. Carl was a career army man and had weathered the second world war as a medic. He now was facing going to Korea. Carl had his own car, and now it became harder to spot Mother as she gave up riding the bus.

Mother began talking of taking us out of the orphanage, and Gerald sensed what was happening as her love for Carl grew.

The year began moving faster it seemed, and Thanksgiving rolled around. Thanksgiving day, 1951 was a clear day, with temperature in the mid sixties. The holidays created an atmosphere like none other. Everyone is happier, food is plentiful, tension is eased. Mrs. Barton had changed ever since her months' absence a year before, and we were all looking forward to a happy holiday season.

At Thanksgiving dinner, Mrs. Barton was sitting at the head of the table, as usual. When the older girls were serving the food, Donald turned around in his seat to look outside, and in the process, bumped a girl with a tray of cranberry sauce, causing her to drop a plate.

"Donald, come here!" said Mrs. Barton.

As he got nearer he lowered his head, like a shamed dog does when it knows its done wrong. Out of nowhere SLAP! Donald went to the floor. His scream was hardly noticeable in the larger room, but I knew it was Donald.

"Get over to your room, and get into bed!"

He stumbled out of the cafeteria and went straight out the larger room to the little boys building. Looking out the larger room, I could see Donald wiping his tears as he hurried along.

We were not allowed in our rooms until that night. After everyone was sleeping I went to Donald's bed. He was still awake and shaking with fear that Mrs. Barton might come back. All my fear of her disappeared. I wrapped my arms around him and told him I'd stay till morning, and if she did come back, I'd protect him. From that moment on the hate built up inside me and ZI knew if I didn't release that tension I would hate her forever.

Three weeks later, just a week before Christmas, I was cleaning up the room I was assigned to. During this, my thoughts of Christmas overtook me. I forgot to tighten the sheet on the beds. I just folded them and got in a hurry trying to finish. At that moment I felt a cold feeling as if I was being watched. Turning around I found myself face to face with Mrs. Barton.

She ripped the covers from one bed, yelling and swinging at me. A glancing blow sent me reeling across one bed. Five years of fearing her and hating her released at once.

SILENT TEARS

"You old witch, I'll kill you!"

I jumped on a bed, grabbing a pillow, and starting swinging and charging Mrs. Barton. The attack caught her off guard. I swung as hard as I could, striking her in the head. She stepped aside and regained the upper hand, slinging me to the floor. I felt pain as her foot crashed into my head. I became a wild animal unafraid of the end results. I found my hands on a chair. ZI lifted it and poised to charge. That old woman became as strong as an ox. Her next blow caught my face, making my nose bleed and I lost my grip on the chair. She picked it up and began to come down on my body as I lay on the floor. But she stopped with her steel eyes glued to mind. She could tell the damage she had caused and as she turned, all energy seemed to drain. Through my dazed condition, I heard a whimpering as of a hurt animal.

"Oh, Lord, what am I doing to these children? Help me, please, somebody help me?"

On my knees all I could see was a pathetic old woman, huddled in a corner and shaking. My pain and suffering disappeared as I pitied this old woman. I knew she couldn't hurt me anymore.

"Mrs. Barton, I'm sorry. Please don't cry."

"Tommy, Tommy. I know I have a problem. I've been to a doctor, and I've been trying to help myself. I knew one day I would come face to face with it. Look at your face. Blood everywhere. Let's clean up and talk."

Like a couple of soldiers after battle, we helped each other to her room. She wiped my face with a warm cloth and gentle hand. The warm rag was removing my hatred and agony of the moment of my victory to overcome all fear.

SILENT TEARS

For the next hour I sat and listened to the story of this old hurt woman. Mrs. Barton was married but had lost her husband, a man she loved very much. She felt cheated and robbed of the love she had lost when he died. All her anger was vented toward the children. Her shame was unbelievable as she unfolded her story to me. The pity of it all. Here I was, only nine years old, really unable to comprehend the true meaning of these moments, but yes, I did understand pain and hurt and sincerity.

LEAVING

The next few months passed very quickly and in May Gerald noticed a letter in Mother's purse addressed to Mr. and Mrs. O. Mason. He knew they were married. In may Mother finally came out and told us. At last we could go home. Mother tried to get us to stay another year by promising to buy us a bicycle each, but we would have none of it. We all cried like babies and she said in the summer we would leave.

In mid-July of 1952 Mother came to get us. Carl had 1952 (Henry J.) automobile, brand new. Mrs. Barton had Donald and me cleaned up and as we waited in the front room of the upstairs hall, she came and told us to hold out our hands. In Donalds she put some change. In mine she put one half dollar, one nickel, one dime, and two pennies. I couldn't believe it! These were probably the very coins she took from me over a three year period. There's no telling how she kept track of them.

"Tommy, thank you, and do come to see me."

We embraced and I had mixed emotions. I remembered all the hate and brutalization I went through but could not help feeling sorry for her and almost loving her. We said all our good-byes and for the last time passed though the large pillars. The sign had been changed to read Children's Home instead of Orphanage Home.

July 1952?

SILENT TEARS

Epilogue

Raymond Aldridge:

Two years after moving from the orphanage I saw him in a housing project in Nashville. We attended Jr. High together, and High School. His claim to fame was playing "Last Date" on the piano at Hume Fogg High School senior day.

Don (Birdnest) Hawkins:

He attended Jr. High with Raymond and me at Highland Heights. His nickname at that time was "Hawkeye".

Douglas Meyers:

His mother lived close to Raymond and when visiting I was able to see both Douglas and his brother. They remained in the home until out of High school.

Bill Smotherman:

The last time I saw him he was still at the orphanage.

Fivers (of the band):

He committed suicide in Nashville in 1964.

Jessie Stewart:

He committed suicide in Nashville by hanging. His note read "Unable to understand life. I am all alone.

Phil Jenkins:

He ran away as the same time as Ralph. He was killed in a car accident in Kentucky in 1959.

Ralph McCarty:

He ran away from the orphanage with his older brother in 1953 for the last time. I saw their pictures in the Nashville paper, where their older brother and his wife said they could live with them...

Gerald Gillespie:

He was married after serving in the military. He and his wife had five children, but are not divorced.

Donald Gillespie:

He was married shortly after finishing High School and has five children.

Tommy Gillespie:

Married and divorced four times. Has two children, both living with him.

Mrs. Barton:

She died in an Old Folks home in Nashville sometime after 1970.

[Need something on Bobby Brewer, Bobby Moon, and John Nag]

"Bobby Moon died in 2007 of cancer. We did visit a few times at reunions, which they no longer have."